LEGACY
HOPE

— ONE FAMILY'S JOURNEY —

LYNN M. MONTGOMERY

WESTBOW
PRESS®
A DIVISION OF THOMAS NELSON
& ZONDERVAN

This book is a work of non-fiction. Unless otherwise noted, the author and the publisher make no explicit guarantees as to the accuracy of the information contained in this book and in some cases, names of people and places have been altered to protect their privacy.

WestBow Press books may be ordered through booksellers or by contacting:

WestBow Press
A Division of Thomas Nelson & Zondervan
1663 Liberty Drive
Bloomington, IN 47403
www.westbowpress.com
844-714-3454

Because of the dynamic nature of the Internet, any web addresses or links contained in this book may have changed since publication and may no longer be valid. The views expressed in this work are solely those of the author and do not necessarily reflect the views of the publisher, and the publisher hereby disclaims any responsibility for them.

Scripture quotations marked ESV taken from The Holy Bible, English Standard Version® (ESV®), Copyright © 2001 by Crossway, a publishing ministry of Good News Publishers. All rights reserved.

ISBN: 978-1-6642-1256-5 (sc)
ISBN: 978-1-6642-1257-2 (e)

Print information available on the last page.

WestBow Press rev. date: 11/27/2020

CONTENTS

DEDICATION

"For I know the plans I have for you, declares the
LORD, plans for wholeness and not for evil, to give
you a future full of hope." (Jeremiah 29:11 ESV)

PREFACE

Trusted with an Assignment

My father, Melvin Montgomery, and his sister, my Aunt Rita Jo (Montgomery) Kendrick, had a common interest of researching names of family ancestors in Missouri and Kentucky. I recall stories of covered wagons and pioneer tales when I was a child. However, I confess, I did not appreciate them then as I do now.

One spring day recently, I sat at the kitchen table with my parents and older brother, Paul. The conversation turned to family history.

This time I listened intently. After going down to the basement, Dad produced pages of records, letters and photos neatly kept in a crowded envelope. He tossed them into the middle of the table and said "Here." My brother gently slid the records to my side of the table as if to say "You know what to do".

Paul knew I had dabbled in writing. What he did not know was that I had prayed for a topic, something new of which to write. In fact, this prayer request had been that very morning. As I do not believe there is such a thing as a coincidence, I took this assignment very seriously.

When I looked at the dates of the records I held in my hand, I was stunned. The earliest dates stretched back into the 1600s; I was certain this was the answer to my prayerful request. But I wanted to write more than a mere listing of names reaching back into time. I wanted to tell the story as completely and honestly as possible, with nothing of significance left out.

Thomas Hagan was the first immigrant family member of my paternal great grandfather, Richard Hagan. He arrived in St. Mary's, Maryland on the Chesapeake Bay in 1662. The settlement was well established by that time as a prosperous colony of tobacco farmers.

My great grandfather Richard was the sixth generation of this family. He died before I was born, but I remember my Great Grandma "Carrie" Belle Hagan. I recall a beaming picture of her surrounded by more great grandchildren than the camera could completely capture.

The family had been Irish Catholics for generations, farmers who had first grown tobacco in the rich Maryland soil; corn in Kentucky soil; and corn, wheat, and oats in Missouri soil. Prosperity was something fought for; nothing had come easily.

Thomas Hagan had survived his indentured servitude for fifty acres of precious Maryland soil. He lived to the ripe age of "seventy odd years" at a time when the life expectancy was much less. He left over 1500 acres at the time of his passing to his wife and nine children.[1]

A little research online taught me that St. Mary's, Maryland is an active archeological site. Historic St. Mary's City had been "found" after it disappeared three centuries ago.[2] So, I cleared my schedule for the fall. I planned a two-week journey to discover the route my branch of the Hagan family had travelled. From Maryland to Missouri, it was a search for freedom from persecution, a desire to worship openly, and the hope of a better life.

ACKNOWLEDGEMENTS

I would like to thank family members before me who painstakingly combed through records that we might all benefit from what they found. For those who lovingly preserved pictures, newspaper clippings, and keepsakes from bibles, reunions, and gatherings, I have tried to share the "wealth". For all who helped me put this together: librarians, historians, and parish members, I owe a debt. For all who listened to my concerns that I had taken on a project beyond my abilities, I thank you for your encouragement. And, finally, for grandchildren and great grandchildren who keep us always looking forward, I am most grateful.

OPPORTUNITY NOT WITHOUT RISK

A BOY, NO MORE THAN TWELVE, TOSSED ABOUT IN THE HOLD of a 17th century sailing vessel. On a journey of weeks that mercilessly turned into months, the monotony of life at sea was surpassed only by the misery. Crushing homesickness was multiplied by the nausea of seasickness. This was interrupted only by the harsh realities of life at sea: a meager, often vermin-infested diet; the danger of disease from humans packed closely; anxiety; stench; and perils of the sea itself.

Much about this young lad is unknown. His survival was not likely. If he lived through the journey, young Thomas would be forced to endure the brutality of new diseases, a new culture, extremely hard work, and the uncertainties his future held.

All those he loved would forever be left behind.

We know he was born in Ireland as evidenced by his name. In the colony of Maryland his surname would be Hagan. That he was once an O'Hagan from Ireland there would be no doubt.

The names he would later give to the acres he painstakingly acquired would confirm this fact. The puzzle that we, his family members, are left with is the circumstances surrounding his departure.

Why had a mere boy left his homeland? It is difficult to believe he would have set out voluntarily.

The English Civil War had caused massive political upheaval around the time Thomas was born, estimated to be 1645. The third English Civil War was the last of the armed conflicts from 1649 to 1651. Ireland was all but destroyed.

After Cromwell's conquest and settlement of Ireland (1649 to 1653) Cromwell did not want yet another war with the Irish. He came up with his own strategy to prevent this from occurring.

Thousands of Irish youth were forced into indentured servitude and some of these were mere children. Between 1652 and 1659 many unfortunate souls were rounded up from across the country as political prisoners. They were forced into servitude and shipped to Barbados and other overseas colonies to work off their debt.[3] Although Thomas had arrived by way of this island, it is not known if he was originally sent there. English ships often made a stop in Barbados en route to the colonies.

While the exact circumstances surrounding his departure are unknown, one thing is certain. Thomas not only survived but thrived in his new life.

The first court record bearing the name of Thomas Hagan is from October, 1662, in Charles County, Maryland. A consignment of sugar from the freight of John Meekes out of Barbados into Virginia had been delivered to a certain resident of Maryland. Young Thomas was the indentured servant of John Meekes. In exchange for transportation to the colony, Thomas would have been provided food, shelter and clothing.

Cheap labor was required to transform the wilderness of the colonies into a cultured society. Of those who answered the call, many were indentured servants. Men as well as women, and some children, took this opportunity for a new life. Some came willingly; some were forced. If they survived the first two years in the colonies, referred to as the "seasoning", there was an opportunity to substantially improve their lives.

A voyage across the Atlantic could take months without sight of land. Social distinctions, so important in England, were brought aboard with the passengers. The hardships of an ocean crossing depended largely upon who you were. Lower ranking passengers were kept in the 'tween deck of a ship. The space was confining; it was crowded with, not only passengers, but supplies and cargo. Thomas, most likely, was rarely allowed on deck.

An indenture usually bound an adult for a period of four to five years. Children were bound until they reached the age of majority. If the venture was taken and won, they were rewarded with their freedom, a new suit of clothes, an axe, two hoes, three barrels of corn, and the rights to fifty acres of land.[4] In the summer of 1662, Thomas was estimated to be seventeen as judged by a deposition he gave in 1715 as "seventy odd years". We can guess that John Meekes was less than honest or simply didn't know Maryland law. He attempted to extend Thomas's servitude with a new indenture dated 12 August 1662. This was invalidated as contrary to a law of the Maryland Assembly and Thomas was declared to be a free man.

MARYLAND;
GOD'S PROVISION

NEARLY FOUR CENTURIES AGO A SMALL GROUP, COMPRISED mostly of Englishmen, left their homeland to establish a settlement in the new American colonies. Owned by the Calvert family, this venture was hoped to not only be a profitable investment, but a means of allowing Catholics to worship freely. Extensive preparations for such a bold journey took more than a year. Of the 140 who made this first journey there were seventeen, mostly wealthy, Catholic men who took along indentured men in their service.

Three of these men were Roman Catholic priests.[5] The remainder of passengers was Protestant. It was the fond hope of the Calvert family to leave behind the religious intolerances of Europe and start fresh in a new colony to be named Maryland.

The hatred between Catholics and Protestants was a raging storm that threatened Europe. The Calverts wanted to leave all of this behind.

The fury was initially fueled by the Inquisition, where those who did not adopt the standards of the Roman Catholic church were put to death as heretics. Later, events of the 15th and 16th centuries brought the hatred to a full boil. The church had become deeply involved with political affairs. There were those who saw this as morally wrong and who sought to end this public role. Other reformers were more concerned about the theological direction of the church, which had drifted over the centuries. The two most prominent reformers who led the Protestant movement were Martin Luther and John Calvin.

Martin Luther, a pastor and professor, aimed his famous "95 Theses" at what he saw as the root of the problem. Once a Catholic priest, he had been excommunicated by Pope Leo X in 1521. He saw the Catholic Church moving away from God's free gift of grace, instead requiring a complex system of indulgences and good works. Luther, by contrast, claimed faith in Jesus as the sinless Lamb of God was what saved a man from his sins. He further insisted that the pope had no authority over what the Catholics called purgatory. God's grace was a free gift that determined eternal life; there was no intermediate step. Otherwise, Jesus's death for our sins was not the perfect sacrifice to atone for sin. Therefore, the Catholic Church did not have the right to sell indulgences which claimed to free a soul trapped in purgatory. Indulgences were often sold to those who had little means to pay and the Catholic Church profited from the sale. At the heart of this fight was the Protestant view that all authority comes from scripture. The Catholic view, that all authority comes from the pope who is infallible, was seen as heresy by the Protestants.

John Calvin was a French lawyer who agreed with Luther's position on justification by faith. He was forced to flee France after his conversion to Protestantism.

In England, the reformation was both political and religious. King Henry VIII was enraged when Pope Clement VII refused to grant him an annulment of his marriage to Catherine of Aragon, his first wife. Divorce was rarely granted unless there was evidence that the marriage was invalid. Henry broke from the pope's authority and established the Anglican Church (the Church of England) with the king of England as the supreme head.[6]

As a Catholic, George Calvert had personal experiences of persecution for his faith. As a boy in England his family could not worship publicly, could not attend English universities, nor could they hold a job in government. The English authorities forced many

Catholics, including George's father, to worship in the Church of England. To avoid persecution and imprisonment, his father had complied. At the age of twelve, George was ordered sent from his home to be educated by a Protestant tutor.[7]

George eventually moved his family to a small colony in Newfoundland, North America. Cecil, his son, was left behind to manage the family business in England. But the Newfoundland colony failed after a severe northern winter.

George later returned to England where he and Cecil negotiated with King Charles I for a charter to establish a colony next to Virginia. The English colonists had discovered that sweet tobacco grew well in the Chesapeake Bay climate. There was great demand for tobacco in England as smoking was both fashionable and addictive. It was hoped that the king would see the financial prospects of the venture and agree to the charter.

After three years, Charles finally agreed to the request. The new colony would be named the Province of Maryland, in honor of the king's Catholic wife, Queen Henrietta Maria.[8]

Cecil Calvert, the first Lord Baltimore, was only twenty-six when he became Maryland's lord proprietor after his father died in 1632. Following his father's wishes, Cecil instituted a policy called liberty of conscience.[9] At a time when Roman Catholicism was condemned in England, the Calverts chose to establish a very liberal policy in Maryland which "tolerated" Christians of other religions.[10]

Cecil needed help finding Catholic families willing to leave the comforts of Europe and settle in his new colony. He made the acquaintance of Father Andrew White, a Jesuit priest (the Society of Jesus) and found him a most willing helper. Father White had gone to school in colleges in England, Spain, and France. He later taught at two universities in France.

Father White enjoyed adventure. He had a keen desire to establish a Catholic mission in Maryland to meet the spiritual needs of the colonists and to convert the Native Americans to Catholicism.

In November, 1633, he and two fellow priests, along with nine indentured servants, prepared for the voyage to what would be Maryland. They were among about 140 who first established the colony.

Father White kept a detailed journal, "Voyage into Maryland" which became an important book of Maryland's early history. The first settlers of Maryland arrived on two ships, the *Ark* and the *Dove*

PROVIDENCE;
ESTABLISHING ST. MARY'S

THE OVERSEA VENTURE TO ESTABLISH A NEW COLONY TOOK four agonizing months. Midway to their intended destination, a terrible storm caused all onboard, crew and passengers, to fear for their lives. Father White recorded that he prayed for God's help, as did many. The winds of the storm blew the ship southward and they were able to rest in Barbados while the ship was repaired.

Before landing in Maryland, one of the ships landed in Virginia. More supplies were loaded and experienced guides like Captain Henry Fleet were brought along.

Fleet had been taken captive and imprisoned for five years among the local natives. Fortunately for all, he had learned the language of his captors during that time. He later made his living as a trader for furs with the natives and as a guide. When Governor Calvert first met the local tribes, Captain Henry Fleet was able to serve as translator.[11]

After sailing up the Potomac River to St. Clement's Island, the English explored and chose a site for settlement. It was there on March 25, 1634 that Father White celebrated the first Catholic Mass in English America. The colonists took communion, followed by a procession of settlers led by the governor. The governor and other officers carried a heavy cross on their shoulders and erected it on the island. They then knelt as Father White recited "The Litany of the Holy Cross".[12] I include it here that the dedication of ancestors may be known. While it has been spoken since, we must imagine it as spoken then: most gratefully, for survival of the journey; penitently, as from souls most humbled by trials; and desperately, as those most in need of guidance:

> "Lord, have mercy. *Lord, have mercy.*
> Christ, have mercy. *Christ, have mercy.*
> Christ, hear us. *Christ, graciously hear us.*
> God the Father of Heaven, *Have mercy on us.*
> God the Son, Redeemer of the world, *Have mercy on us.*
> God the Holy Spirit, our Advocate, *Have mercy on us.*
> Holy Trinity, one God, *Have mercy on us.*
> Holy Cross on which the Lamb of God was offered, *save us, O Holy Cross.*
> Hope of Christians, *Save us O Holy Cross.*
> Pledge of the Resurrection of the dead, *save us, O Holy Cross.*
> Shelter of persecuted innocence, *save us, O Holy Cross.*
> Way of those who have gone astray, *save us, O Holy Cross,*
> Consolation of the poor, *save us, O Holy Cross,*

Restraint of the powerful, *save us, O Holy Cross.*
Refuge of sinners, *save us, O Holy Cross.*
Terror of demons, sav*e us, O Holy Cross.*
Guide of youth, *save us, O Holy Cross.*
Hope of the hopeless, *save us, O Holy Cross.*
Safeguard of childhood, *save us, O Holy Cross"*

With the same refrain, spoken after the priest, it continues:

"Strength of manhood, Last hope of the aged,
Wisdom of the foolish, Liberty of slaves,
Knowledge of the ignorant, Sure rule of life,
Heralded by the prophets, Preached by the apostles,
Glory of martyrs, Study of hermits, Chastity of
virgins, Joy of priests, Foundation of the Church,
Salvation of the world, Support of the weak,
Medicine of the sick, Bread of the hungry, Fountain
of those who thirst, who takes away the sins of the
world. *Spare us, O Lord.*
Lamb of God, who takes away the sins of the world,
Hear us, O Lord.
Lamb of God, who takes away the sins of the world,
Have mercy on us.
Lord have mercy, Christ have mercy, Lord have
mercy.
We adore You, O Christ and we bless You, *because
by Your Holy Cross You have redeemed the world.*
Behold the Cross of the Lord. By the power of the
Cross of Our Lord Jesus Christ
May the power of evil be vanquished
The Lion of the tribe of Judah, The Root of David,
Has conquered. Alleluia. Amen.
Let us pray:
O God, who for the redemption of the world, was
pleased to be born in a stable

and to die upon a Cross;
O Lord Jesus Christ, by Your sufferings, which we,
Your unworthy servants,
call to mind: by the Holy Cross and by Your death,
deliver us from the pains of hell and conduct us to
Paradise
as You did the good thief who was crucified
with You.
Who lives and reigns eternally in Heaven."[13]

ESTABLISHING
ST. MARY'S

N ATIVE AMERICAN PEOPLE IN THE CHESAPEAKE BAY AREA
were known as Yaocomaco, pronounced Yuh-kahm'-muh-ko,
which meant a place of several dwellings. Most fortunately for the
new settlers, they had a village that occupied both sides of the
St. Mary's River, including the land that eventually became St.
Mary's. After negotiating with local Native American leaders, the
settlers acquired part of a village to live in while a fort and houses
were built. In exchange, the colonists were to provide protection
from enemies which, at times, had been a problem.

The Yaocomaco taught the settlers how to prepare the land
and make fields to grow corn and other crops. These skills were
essential to the survival of the English. The relationship between
the Yaocomaco and the colonists was peaceful.[14]

Catholics began as a minority in Maryland and would always
continue to be so. There were also other religious groups who took
advantage of the liberal atmosphere of tolerance for faith. These
included Quakers and Presbyterians.

The Society of Jesus, also known as Jesuits, was a major investor
in the Maryland colony. Eventually, this group earned possession
of thousands of acres of land. Cecil Calvert granted a manor,
1000 acres of land, to any man who brought five male servants to
Maryland. This was a long-enduring English system of property
ownership.[15] The Jesuits also served as the principal clergy during

the colonial period. Between 1634 and 1645, the population of the colony had grown to between 500 and 600 settlers. The entire focus of the colony was growing tobacco for export to England.[16]

Tobacco was the medium of exchange in Maryland, a system of debits and credits. This was essentially a cashless colony. Many English adventurers came to Maryland to make their fortune in tobacco. Smoking was fashionable for all classes in England, rich and poor. Because of this demand, the planters were growing their own version of American gold. A hogshead (round wooden cask, the cardboard box of the time) filled with dried tobacco weighed about 400 lbs. A carpenter would expect a daily wage of 20 pounds of tobacco. A pair of shoes cost 12 pounds. A cow could cost as much as 1000 lbs of tobacco. The amount paid or owed was dependent on how much English money was needed to buy a specific amount of tobacco.[17]

A final settlement of Thomas Hagan's estate was made on 13 June, 1717 by Mary Hagan, the Executrix. It included a disbursement of 500 lbs. of tobacco for the funeral sermon.[18]

THE BRICK
CHAPEL

Reconstructed brick chapel, Historic St. Mary's, Maryland,
first Catholic chapel in English America

As toleration of Catholics increased in England, the Jesuit priests in Maryland eventually felt confident enough to have a brick chapel built. In 1667, an impressive red brick church was built in the shape of a cross. It was 54 feet long, 57 feet across the arms, and 28 feet wide. The floor featured imported stone and the roof was covered with tile. Symbolically, this chapel represented the flowering of the idea of religious toleration in Maryland.[19] This chapel served the colonists in Maryland until 1704.

This very church would have been the chapel that, no doubt, Thomas and his family attended. By 17th century standards it was a monumental structure. However, political turmoil demanded that it eventually be torn down. It was later reconstructed as a symbol of religious freedom established first in the New World.[20]

When the tide changed, Maryland passed an "Act against Popery" in 1704 which closed all Catholic churches.

WHAT IS KNOWN
OF THOMAS HAGAN
AND FAMILY

C OURT RECORDS AND CHURCH RECORDS FROM THE 17TH century have survived since American colonial times. As others have been able to trace this lineage, that has made this work possible. In addition, archeological research can fill in some details to tell us what it known.

Not until 1670 did Thomas acquire his fifty acres for his servitude. Maryland law demanded that he pay to have his land surveyed before he could take possession. He did so. At the same time he married a woman we only know as "Mary". Mary's surname cannot be directly traced, although there has been speculation that it may have been Aisquith.[21] Another known fact is that young Thomas found a wife when few women were available in the colony.

The first tract of land that he acquired, Thomas called "Newcastle". This probably reflected some homesickness and gives a hint as to where he may have come from. Newcastle was an Irish port city at the time of Cromwell's conquest which still exists today.

Only two years later, a tract of 150 acres was surveyed by him. He named this land "Correct Measure". One can only wonder if "correct measure" referred to what he felt was truly due him for his endured indenture. In 1678 "St. James" was surveyed for him, originally 200 acres; It was later surveyed for 317 acres. Another 650 acres was surveyed for him, called "Good Intent", in 1695. By the time of his death, this former servant had acquired by his own efforts over 1500 acres of land.[22]

Thomas and Mary had nine children as mentioned in his final will and testament. James is presumed to be the eldest, possibly born in 1671. To James he left 350 acres of "Good Intent". To his other four sons he left land, although less in acreage. To four of his five daughters he left a token ten shillings each, indicating he had already provided for them in a dowry. But to his fifth daughter, possibly the eldest, he left 100 acres of land. All had married. His personal estate, including 300 acres of "St. James" which he bequeathed to his wife Mary "during her natural life and after her decease to my son William Hagan". William is presumed to be the youngest son.[23]

A WOMAN'S WORLD

A WOMAN'S LIFE IN THE COLONIES WAS WROUGHT WITH HARD WORK. As there were few women in the early years of the Maryland colony, they were much in demand as wives.

A woman cared for cows, poultry, and the kitchen garden. She milked the cow, churned the butter, and salted and dried meat after butchering. She did the cooking, cleaning, and sometimes worked in the fields. It was a woman's job to grind the dry kernels of corn using an iron pestle inside a wooden mortar. The chore was monotonous and exhausting. It was so despised that some indentured servants added a clause to their contract that specified they would not grind corn. By 1639 a mill existed on Mill Creek, a fifteen minute walk from St. Mary's.[24] Mary may have sent corn to the mill for grinding.

Mary would not have had to weave cloth or dip candles, unlike other women in colonial New England. Marylanders imported almost all manufactured goods from England. As an English ship would arrive regularly, it would bring needed goods when it was time to pick up the costly tobacco. This included dry goods, cloth, candles, tools, oil, pots, pans, pottery, ceramics, glass, and wool blankets.

Making these items would have taken time and energy from supplying the needs of those busy growing tobacco. There was such a fervor to grow tobacco that laws had to be passed in Maryland to ensure that tobacco farmers grew enough corn to feed themselves and their families.[25]

Caring for the Hagan children was Mary's responsibility. After the age of six, colonial children had too many chores to do to have much free time for play. They would gather firewood, carry buckets of water, mend clothes, prepare food, and gather eggs.[26]

Catholic families tended to be large. The family was the necessary social unit of the times as well as the security for old age. Many women died in childbirth and men would remarry quickly out of sheer need. Children often did not survive until adulthood.

A trip to the St. Mary's archeological site taught me more about life in those times. It was certainly life with few comforts. Only one "privy" (outhouse) was discovered in all of the St. Mary's site. Emptying chamber pots was a daily chore. Garbage was simply tossed out the front door. Most homes had cows, pigs, and chickens. The only fences were those around the garden.

Women wore a vest and a petticoat covered by an apron. The shift beneath, which was long-sleeved and extended down to her calves, doubled as nightclothes. Some type of head covering was worn at all times.[27]

Fifteen to thirty people lived in a two story home on a typical tobacco farm. Indentured servants sometimes slept with other family members, often children. People slept four to a bed, which was a mattress stuffed with hay. A featherbed was a great luxury. Fire was a constant threat to the home, and many homes had a fire plan.

In 17th century Maryland, women were greatly outnumbered by men. Death rates were high. As a result, a female who was freed from her indentured servitude would not remain single for long.

A MAN'S WORLD

HISTORICAL RECORDS SHOW THAT ANY MARYLANDER WHO had a couple of acres grew tobacco. Native Americans were the first to smoke tobacco, using pipes. The English soon developed a taste for it and the sweet weed became much in demand in Europe. It was a crop that was highly profitable and one that thrived in the soil and climate of Virginia and Maryland.

Tobacco farming was year-round work that required a great deal of effort. In February the land was cleared and soil made ready. Land was cleared by cutting the bark around each tree so it would die. Everything under the trees was then burned. A hoe was used to break up the soil and work in the ash and coal. The soil was then formed into small hills. "Planters" and their servants worked long and hard, at least 12 hours a day, 6 days a week doing back-breaking work. By 1680, each worker was expected to tend approximately 10,000 plants.[28]

The seeds were started in the spring. The seedlings were later transplanted to knee-high hills where they remained until leaves were fully mature. During the summer, the tobacco was weeded and the lowest leaves of the plants were pulled off. This forced the plant's nutrients into the upper leaves making them grow larger and increasing their value at market. In autumn the stalks were harvested and hung until dry, about four to six weeks. A daily check was done for signs of mold that could destroy the leaves. Finally, the men bundled the dried leaves into wooden casks called hogsheads. Transport fees for shipping overseas were charged by number of hogsheads rather than by weight, so planters stuffed them as full as possible. As a fully packed hogshead weighed about 400 pounds, they were best moved by rolling to the nearest waterway for transport. Tobacco farms were usually located along rivers or inlets.

Rolling a hogshead was a dangerous task as it could easily crush an arm or leg.[29]

Tobacco rapidly exhausted the soil in which it was grown; it could be grown for three to five years before the soil was too depleted to produce a profitable tobacco crop. The land would then be used for corn for two or three years. Afterward, it had to lie fallow for twenty years before tobacco could profitably be grown on it again. The need to constantly acquire more land became apparent.

Settlements in Maryland developed along the edges of the Chesapeake Bay which could be navigated by ships.[30]

IGNATIUS HAGAN

I N RECENT YEARS, ARCHEOLOGIST HAVE DISCOVERED, IN THE soil, medallions that were worn in the early years of St. Mary's. One of these medallions that differs from those found in other colonies is the medallion of St. Ignatius of Loyola. Ignatius, a frequent name in Hagan ancestry, was the founder of the Jesuits (Society of Jesus).[31]

Our Ignatius was the seventh out of nine children born to Thomas and Mary. He was the third son. Born about 1686 in Charles County, Maryland, he was the next ancestor in my great grandfather Hagan's line of descent. He was known as Ignatius "Planter" Hagan, no doubt a reference to his occupation.

Ignatius was about thirty years of age when he inherited 265 acres of land from his father. By this time, he had married Rebecca Lowe who was born in 1690. Rebecca was the daughter of Major John Lowe from England who was a Major in the colonial Troops of St. Marys' Company. Rebecca's father was a member of the Church of England; he died prior to their marriage.

One can only wonder if John Lowe would have objected to his daughter marrying a Catholic. However, in his will, he left Rebecca 150 acres of land, "The Garden". The will specified that she would not receive the property if she married before the age of fifteen.[32]

Rebecca gave birth to their first son, William, about 1712, and their second son, Thomas, about 1716. They went on to have a total of eight children. Their youngest son, Joseph, was born about

1730. After the death of Rebecca, Ignatius had a second marriage to Magdalen Thompson.

The will of Ignatius Hagan is dated 15 October, 1765. He was 79 years of age. He divided his assets among his children, leaving two of his daughters "one shilling of sterling". Dowries were given at the time of marriage. He left 100 acres of land to his wife Magdalen "as long as she lives and after her decease to my loving son Joseph Hagan".

SLAVERY GAINS
A FOOTHOLD

W HILE SLAVERY EXISTED IN EARLY 17ᵀᴴ CENTURY MARYLAND, the status of Africans was not well defined. They were as likely to be indentured servants as to be slaves. [33]

Matthias de Sousa was one of the first men of African descent to arrive with the Ark and the Dove in 1634. Although his surname is Portuguese, his birthplace is unknown. De Sousa was an indentured servant to the Jesuit priests who first sailed to Maryland, one of nine. He later became a free man and a mariner.[34]

In the first half of the 17th century, it was cheaper to buy an indentured European than an enslaved African who might cost five times as much. If the "investment" died an untimely death due to hardship or disease, the owner lost less money. It wasn't until the latter half of the 17th century that laws were passed making enslavement a lifetime condition for Africans. Still, some masters set a length of time for servitude.

In time, indentured servants were replaced by slaves in the tobacco fields. A dark chapter of American history had begun.[35]

THE AMERICAN REVOLUTION

WHEN THE AMERICAN REVOLUTIONARY WAR BEGAN IN 1775 the newly-formed country did not have a regular army. Instead, each colony defended itself with a militia of local men. With few exceptions, any male age 16 up to age 60 was expected to participate. By 1776, George Washington had an army of 20,000 men. Two-thirds were regular army and one-third were from colonial militia.

The newly formed government of the colonies simply did not have enough money to pay soldiers. With expectation of victory, bounty land was to be awarded both as an incentive and a reward for serving. Obviously, no land could be actually awarded until the British were defeated.

Land allotted was determined by rank and time in service.

Some of the smaller states did not have enough bounty land for the policy. Instead, reserves in the western, not yet settled areas were selected. There was an added benefit to this policy; the government needed ex-soldiers along the frontier to protect settlers. Settlers in those areas were facing increasing uprisings from Native American tribes who could clearly see that their way of life was being threatened.[36]

After the Victory at Yorktown in 1781, army veterans were encouraged to claim their land. If they perished in the war, an heir could claim the land. Land grants could also be sold.

Land plots were numbered and drawn by lot. Virginia established a court of inquiry to determine which pioneers had the best rights to particular lands. The court could also reject a claim if an "Oath of Fidelity and Allegiance" had not been taken during the Revolutionary War.

There were many problems with these claims. Among them were spelling of names as many were illiterate, replication of names, and fraud. There was also much ignorance and stubbornness. Needless to say, not all who thought they might be able to claim land were able to do so.[37]

Before 1792, Kentucky was part of Virginia. Some members of the Hagan family had moved to Virginia in an attempt to escape the persecutions and excessive taxation of Maryland.

THE WEST; DOOR
OF HOPE

MARYLAND'S FIRST EXPERIMENT IN RELIGIOUS TOLERATION only persevered as long as England would allow. The Glorious Revolution of 1688 permanently established Parliament as the ruling power of England. It resulted in a royal governor taking charge of Maryland from the Calvert family by 1692. State government was restored to them in 1715 after the Calverts became Protestant. In 1699 a test oath requirement excluded Catholics from government positions. In 1702 the Church of England was made the official church of Maryland.

From 1704 to 1709, Catholics were no longer allowed to practice their religion openly. The number of Catholics in Maryland at that time was about 3000 out of a population of 34,000. Half of them lived in the St. Mary's region.

While times had been prosperous in seventeenth century Maryland, the economic situation was desperate by the mid eighteenth century. The price of tobacco fluctuated widely and all ranks of people were in a state of bankruptcy. To add to this strife, in 1756 the assembly provided for a double tax on Roman Catholic landholders. Catholics labored under these many difficulties.[38] Some of the names for Hagan land revealed the changing times, from "Hagan's Chance" to "Hagan's Folly" and, finally, "Hagan's Strife".[39]

Around the time the American Revolution was ending, Europe was undergoing a religious upheaval called the "Great

Awakening". This unrest pushed those undergoing persecution as heretics to leave their native lands and come to the colonies. At the same time the French Revolution caused many French Catholics to escape to the New World. As Catholic beliefs were not well tolerated elsewhere in the American colonies, many took refuge in Maryland. I found an incredible number of Catholic surnames repeated from Maryland to Kentucky to Missouri. Most of them were not Irish, but also European. English, Welsh, Scottish, French, German, and Dutch surnames were also represented. What kept them together was what they had in common; it was their Catholic faith fleeing persecution.

Daniel Boone had blazed a trail through the Cumberland Gap to Kentucky in 1775. This overland route was named The Wilderness Road. It was steep and narrow, and could only be traveled on horseback or on foot. Most likely to be dangerous, it was almost certain to attract the hostilities of tribes of Native Americans But it had opened up the new Western Frontier, including the land of Kentucky, although at what could be enormous cost.[40]

THE MARYLAND
LEAGUE

IN 1785 A GROUP OF CATHOLIC FAMILIES OF SCOTTISH, IRISH, and English descent agreed to migrate across the Allegany Mountains for a new life in Kentucky. They were motivated by the opportunity for land as well as the desire to practice their religion without restrictions from government. Known as the "Maryland League", they intended to establish a community large enough to be given a priest of their own.

Ignatius "Planter" Hagan died in 1765 when his son Joseph, our next ancestor, was about 35 years of age. Joseph's cousin, James Hagan, died in 1775. James left behind a spunky widow, Monica Johnson Hagan. Not one to miss an opportunity, Monica was part of this league and is listed among those who first made the journey. Monica along with three of her sons, approximately ages 29, 25, and 21 decided to move westward. Four or possibly five daughters also made the journey, the youngest about 10 years of age

Monica's eldest son, James Jr., quite possibly served in The Revolutionary War. There is a Revolutionary War record of a James Hagan of Charles County, Maryland. If so, he enlisted in the Charles County, Maryland militia in 1776 a year after his father died. He served from 1776 until about 1781.[41] There is much repetition of many names such as James, Thomas, Joseph, etc. which makes preciseness difficult. But, he is believed to be the same James Hagan of Nelson County, Kentucky who later applied for an army pension.[42] James Jr, most likely had land to claim from his time of Revolutionary War service.

Originally, 60 families, all Catholics from Maryland, pledged to move to Kentucky within a specified period as circumstances permitted. John Carroll, who was the Catholic Bishop of Baltimore, promised to send them clergy for their spiritual needs if they stayed in close proximity of each other.[43] It is difficult to ask land-needy farmers to live in close proximity. Catholic priests in early America spent more time in the saddle than the pulpit as they journeyed from one family to the next.

The first group of 25 families left Maryland in 1785. They traveled by land to Pittsburgh. There they bought or built flatboats to go down the Ohio River while the rivers were swollen from the winter rains. Timing was essential.[44]

These early travelers were exposed to extraordinary sufferings; they had to meet them with extraordinary courage. They left all comforts behind, as well as friends and family, with virtually no prospects of seeing loved ones again.

THE "ARK"

F LATBOAT TRAVEL WAS RELATIVELY NEW IN 1785. IT HAD become essential as there were few overland roads. In time, a booming flatboat-building business sprang up along the rivers. These less-than-reliable boats were called by many names, including "Kentucky boats" or "arks".

At a basic level, a flatboat was no more than a floating box. It was a rectangular, flat-bottomed boat built for short term use. They were built without keels, which made them much less structurally sound than a regular boat. They were also much more difficult to steer with oars. A typical size for families going west was 16 ft. wide by 55 ft. long. There was a pen in the rear for livestock, and a cabin in front for the family. A sandbox fireplace often served for a cooking fire.

A flatboat could be disassembled upon arrival at the destination and the lumber would be used for building shelter.

Families had to pack wisely for the trip. Food such as cornmeal and bacon, packed in barrels, was needed. Other essential items would have been farm equipment, seeds for planting, carpentry tools, and livestock including oxen for clearing timber and plowing. Needed household items included surgical instruments, needles, thread, and bedding. The family also needed items for weaponry as attacks by native tribes had been reported and were expected.

The only book that would have been allowed to take up needed space was the family Bible. In it were recorded family births, deaths, and marriages.

The settlers faced danger all along the way, including hidden sandbars in the river, mishaps when trying to steer, and poor construction from purchasing a "lemon". In time, the rivers were littered with abandoned flatboats.

The boats were built like floating forts with only one small door in case of attack. The walls were pierced with holes through which guns could be fired.[45]

The first settlers of the Maryland League arrived at Goodwin's Station, near Boston, Kentucky. This was the fort nearest their destination, the land near Pottinger's Creek in Nelson County. The women and children were left at Goodwin Station and the able-bodied men went on to the site of their future homes, about fifteen miles south of the station.

They were followed in the next year by another group of the league who located in the same neighborhood. A third band of Catholic emigrants arrived in 1787 and settled in the same area. While on their journey they were fired upon by a Native American tribe and at least one man was severely wounded.[46]

French Trappist Monks eventually joined the Maryland League in this location to increase the strength of the Catholic faith in America.

JOSEPH HAGAN

Memorial Marker for Catholic pioneers of Maryland League
at Pottinger Creek, Nelson County, Kentucky

JOSEPH HAGAN, OUR NEXT ANCESTOR, WAS 55 YEARS OF AGE when the Maryland League was formed. We know he made the journey from Maryland to the new frontier because he died in 1809 in Nelson, County Kentucky. He was married to Mary Ann King who was 14 years younger. They had 12 children, the last one born in 1787.

Joseph and Mary's youngest child was two years old when cousins, (another) Ignatius and James's widow, Monica, and families started their perilous trek westward. This may explain why Joseph and family made the journey at a later time.

Joseph took the Oath of Allegiance in March, 1778. These Catholics did not fight but pledged their sympathies to the cause of the Revolution. Persecution against Catholics by the local Maryland government was possibly seen as more intense than that from the English Crown.

It is possible that Joseph's eldest son, James Alexius (who often signed his name Electious), may have made an advance trip to Kentucky to secure a homestead when he was in his early twenties. Joseph refers to tobacco left with him by Electious (James Alexius) to be sold. Joseph disposed of his property and left for Nelson County by 1792. [47]

By then, Joseph's youngest child, (yet another) Ignatius, was five.

MEETING SPIRITUAL
NEEDS ON THE
FRONTIER

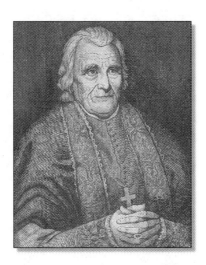

Bishop Benedict Flaget

THE CATHOLICS OF THE MARYLAND LEAGUE WERE TOLD BY
Bishop John Carroll that they would be responsible for
supporting the priesthood sent to Nelson County. As approximately
a third of the Catholic families of Maryland eventually made the
move to this new frontier, they were in sufficient number to do so.

Without a doubt, the first priests to serve in this area faced
enormous challenges. They lived in huts, had little food, traveled

on foot or by boat, and made long rides on horseback through the wilderness from cabin to cabin. To reach a family in need the ministering clergy often crossed rivers in bad weather. Disease and exhaustion took its toll.

Father Maurice Whelan was the first to arrive, an Irishman who had served in the Revolutionary War. He found the Catholic community widely scattered and he struggled in his role. Father Whelan served three years and returned to Maryland in 1790.

That same year, Father Whelan was followed by Father William de Rohan. He would be the one who oversaw the building of the first Catholic Church in Kentucky, a log cabin structure. He later taught school at New Hope.

Father Barrieres of France came to Kentucky in 1793, but left in 1794, unable to endure the hardships of the wilderness.

Father Stephen Badin, Father David Bordeaux, and Father Benedict Flaget, natives of France, met up and sailed together for the United States. Their lives and studies had been interrupted by the French Revolution. Father Badin finished his studies at St. Mary's Seminary in Baltimore in 1793; he was the first priest ordained in the United States.

Father Badin was in Nelson and Washington Counties, Kentucky, serving the Catholic pioneers by 1797. He was approximately 29 years of age at the time of his arrival. His first helper was Father Michael Fournier who also left France because of the Revolution. Father Fournier ruptured a blood vessel and died in 1813.

Father John Thayer came to Kentucky in 1799. However, his political views, which he freely expressed, were not welcomed by most of his parishioners. Father Thayer had a great devotion to the cause of the slaves. Catholics, mostly, saw slavery as a necessary evil. Some of them were slave holders. Slaves were provided with religious instruction, and were baptized and married in religious rites. They were referred to as "servants" and were buried in the parish cemetery without discrimination. However, human kindness by masters, although expected, could not be guaranteed.[48] Matters between Father Thayer and his parish could not be resolved and he left Kentucky in 1799.

That same year, Father Anthony Salmon arrived at the home of Father Badin. Father Salmon saw the need for well-instructed laity and he sought to teach catechism to the children and servants. His ministry was short but fruitful. He died after a fall from his horse when he had been in Kentucky only ten months.

It was Father Badin who bore the greater part of the mission work. He spent his life trying to improve spiritual conditions, relieve suffering, and console the dying. After twenty years in Kentucky he left for France in 1819. He later returned in 1828 and continued his work until his death in 1853.[49]

Father Badin eventually welcomed another well-traveled Frenchman and friend, Bishop Benedict Joseph Flaget, to his humble home. Bishop Flaget had been sent, most reluctantly on his part, by Bishop John Carrol of Baltimore to become the bishop of a new frontier diocese. Initially, he was overwhelmed by the assignment which covered the areas of Kentucky and Tennessee. However, he also had temporary jurisdiction over an area much more vast.

Bishop Flaget was nearly fifty years of age when he timidly accepted the responsibility the Pope had thrust upon him. The hardships of the Kentucky wilderness were made all the worse by his frustration with the language barrier with the settlers. But Benedict Joseph Flaget, was an overcomer, by all reports. His history as a priest in America had already included two smallpox epidemics among settlers and Native Americans. He became ill while ministering to the needs of others, although he eventually recovered. Likewise, Father Flaget caught Yellow Fever when he traveled to Cuba, along with two colleagues, to establish a college. Not one to waste an opportunity, he used his recovery time to learn Spanish. While in Cuba, he made the acquaintance of Louis Phillippe of France, who arrived while in exile. Flaget befriended him, a kindness which Louis Phillipe returned when he ascended the throne of France as king.[50]

EUROPEAN CULTURE
ON THE FRONTIER

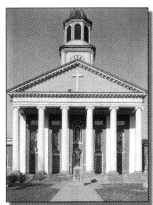

Basilica of St. Joseph's Proto-Cathedral in Bardstown, Kentucky

WITHIN A FEW YEARS AFTER BISHOP FLAGET'S ARRIVAL, THE cornerstone was laid for a massive cathedral which took three years to complete. To obtain pledges to build the Cathedral, a list was prepared and passed around to the members of the different congregations of the diocese. The settlers pledged to give money, materials, or services toward the construction.

Construction included felling massive trees for the structure's pillars and hauling wagons of sand from rivers to make cement. Over one million bricks were made and used in the construction of walls which are 32 inches thick. Two fireplaces on either side of the church were the only sources of heat at the time of construction.

LYNN M. MONTGOMERY

This was the first Catholic Cathedral west of the Allegheny Mountains. It still stands today, known as a Proto-(first) Cathedral. It currently serves as a parish church.

The inside of the cathedral was not fully complete until 1823. Many of the original oil paintings and interior decorations were donated from Europe. King Louis Phillipe of France returned favor to his friend who had been with him in his time of trouble, Bishop Flaget. He sent several original oil paintings by Van Dyck, Murillo, and other well-known artists of the time. Others who donated artwork were King Francis I of the Two Sicilies, and Pope Leo XII. The paintings included "The Crucifixion", "Descent of the Holy Ghost", "St. Peter in Chains" and "St. John the Baptist".[51]

This ornate setting was the center of worship for struggling farmers of simple means. Providence had ordained that these eyes would behold the same majesty as upper class heads of Europe.

JAMES ALEXIUS HAGAN (AND THE DIFFERENT SPELLINGS)

JAMES ALEXIUS HAGAN, NEXT IN THE LINE OF DESCENT, WAS THE ELDEST of twelve children of Joseph Hagan. Born in 1766 in Maryland, he was in his mid- twenties when he made the move to Kentucky. He married Susannah Ann Gwynn, born in 1779, who had also made the same journey in 1799. She was twenty years old when they married. They had eight children, four boys and four girls between 1805 and 1828. One son, Alfred, was ordained as a Catholic priest in 1840. He died of malaria while in his thirties.

James Alexius and Susannah Gwynn Hagan are both buried in the cemetery at St. Joseph's in what is now Bardstown, Kentucky.

A puzzling fact to me was the last name on their headstone. Everything correlates as being distinctly them except the spelling of their last name, Hagan. It is spelled Hagen. Was this an error on the part of the one who lettered the headstone?

James Alexius is also known as Alexius, but he signed his name Electious in other records.[52] The headstone for Alexius and Susannah distinctly spells their last name as Hagen, not Hagan. I first considered that, perhaps, this might be another couple. But the dates were too compelling. And how many Susannah Gwynn Hagans buried at St. Joseph's could there have been who died in 1852, exactly 12 days after her husband?

So, I researched the problem from another angle. Could the change of spelling have been intentional?

While Hagan is a distinctively Irish spelling, Hagen could be a German, Dutch, or Danish surname. Was this spelling accidental or was it to eliminate discrimination they might have faced?

The Irish were still a minority in Kentucky in the mid 1800's. A farmer with eight children might have done whatever necessary to provide for them.

In 1845 Ireland suffered a devastating Potato Blight which caused widespread famine. As Ireland was still a land of poor tenant farmers ruled as a colony of Great Britain, potatoes had been a staple in the diet. This destructive fungus caused many Irish to desperately look for a new opportunity.

By 1850, half a million Irish had arrived in America. Desperately poor, unskilled, and unable to speak English, they huddled in cities where they took jobs in menial labor. They suffered from starvation and diseases such as cholera. Because of this, and because unskilled workers feared being put out of work by the Irish who would work for less, they were not well liked by American society. As they were almost all Catholic, some Protestants feared they were under the control of the pope and therefore could not be patriotic Americans. As anti-Irish and anti-Catholic sentiment grew, ads for jobs or housing routinely ended with the slogan "No Irish Need Apply".

A political party was founded in the 1850's and nicknamed the "Know-Nothing Party"; it was intent on preventing Irish immigration.

The Irish in America were treated badly during these years. It wasn't until after the Civil War where large numbers of Irish fought bravely that this sentiment began to change.[53]

FREE LAND IN
SPANISH AMERICA

I N THE 1790'S A SIGNIFICANT NUMBER OF KENTUCKY SETTLERS moved further west to, what was then, Spanish territory. It is now Missouri. These settlers were offered that which was hard for a Catholic farmer to refuse: free land, no taxes and religious freedom. This offer was especially attractive to settlers in Kentucky who could not obtain clear title to land. However, in 1800, the Spanish secretly sold the land back to France. The U.S. then purchased the land from France in 1803.[54]

Migration of Catholics into what is now Perry County, Missouri began at this time. The Catholics of Kentucky had been noticed by a Spanish Commandant living near what is now St. Genevieve, Missouri. These Catholic famers were viewed as prospective settlers for Spanish America. Spain was in hopes of having Catholic families settle its land.

Joseph Fenwick, a Kentuckian, and head of his family, was invited to bring himself and his son, a doctor, as well as other American Catholics to settle this Spanish Territory. Joseph set out with 25 other families and seventy slaves, to arrive in 1797. However, the land they settled was not good farm land and the settlers soon drifted elsewhere.[55]

Although Joseph Hagan, father of James Alexius, was buried in Kentucky, it seems that he also made the journey to the Spanish dominion west of the Mississippi, now Missouri. Joseph obtained a land grant of 640 acres by 1803.[56] He was nearing 70 when he made this journey, apparently to and from. His wife and his sons Edward, Wilford and James Aquilla, as well as a daughter, Christina, eventually settled in the same area he had claimed. They are buried in Perry County, Missouri.

MISSOURI GAINS STATEHOOD

MISSOURI APPLIED FOR STATEHOOD AS A SLAVE STATE PRIOR to the Civil War. At that time there were already eleven "free" states and eleven "slave" states which guaranteed balance of power in the Senate. This balance was threatened by the admission of a twelfth slave state.

Although the country was in agreement that westward lands should be settled, there was a boiling kettle of emotions over the question of slavery. Many did not want to allow Missouri the "slave state" option. However, the Federal government had not been allowed to determine the status of any previous state. What became known as "The Missouri Compromise" was finally settled upon.

Missouri became a state in 1821, admitted as a "slave state" the same year Maine was admitted as a "free state".

Farmers saw Missouri as fertile land for a comparatively nominal price where one could, if one chose to, own a slave. Farmers in Kentucky saw it as an opportunity. Catholic farmers coming to Missouri saw it as an opportunity with a nearby church and community with shared values.

FIELDER IGNASIUS HAGAN

FIELDER IGNASIUS HAGAN WAS THE SIXTH CHILD BORN TO James Alexius Hagan and Susannah Gwynn Hagan. He was the third son. While his name may have referenced his occupation as a farmer, it seems to have been his legal name. The spelling of his middle name seems to differentiate him from all the other family members with the name Ignatius.

Fielder's uncles, Edward, Wilford, and James Aquilla were among those who had acquired a Spanish land grant in an area along the Mississippi, in what is now Perry County Missouri. To establish their "ownership" the men often built a basic shack as proof of occupancy and planted peach stones or apple seeds before returning to get their families.

These land grants were only legal if later confirmed by the general colonial government of New Orleans. In the end, anyone who could show possession of his land by occupation or cultivation prior to 1804 was approved. However, only thirteen such cases were approved.[57] This area became another center of Catholicism with an active community of faith.

Having relatives in another Catholic community was probably great incentive to make a move should a better opportunity present itself.

In 1825 several Catholic priests from the St. Louis area travelled north to establish a Catholic Mission on the present site of Indian Creek in Monroe County, Missouri. At the time of their arrival there wasn't a town, but after a church was built, a few rugged Catholics decided to move to the area[58]. Among them was a German shop owner by the name of August Schwenke[59]. However, the name "Schwenke" proved difficult for most to pronounce or to spell so he went by "Swinkey". "Swinkey", as the locals called it, eventually became, and still is, the unofficial name of the community. Officially, it is St. Stephen's Parish, Indian Creek, Missouri. It would prove to be an enduring Catholic community that survived the Civil War as well as destruction of the church by a cyclone and later by a fire. Each time the community rallied and rebuilt. It is an active parish today.

The first church was built of logs and was located on the site which is now part of the old cemetery. The first resident priest was Father Peter Paul Lefevere who began his work in 1833.[60] The first death recorded in the cemetery is 1837.[61]

Log cabins at this time were rough but sturdy. Some had puncheon floors but many had dirt floors. The puncheon floor was made of large logs split in two with the flat surfaces facing upward. Splintery they were, but at least the flooring was off the ground. These cabins did not have windows, but holes covered over with greased paper to let light in. The one door had a latch with a latch string usually made of deer thong.[62]

"Cabin raisings" were community events. No one waited for an invitation to help. A house fire might cause a family to be in immediate need of shelter; a community of helpful neighbors was essential.

Fielder was born in Nelson County, Kentucky in 1815. He married Harriet N. Smith in 1838, when he was 23 and she was 25. In January of 1851, Harriet gave birth to their eighth child, a girl. At this time their family consisted of girls ages 12, 11, and 8; twin boys who were 6 years old; two more boys ages 4 and 2; and the baby girl. According to family notes, when the twins, George Washington and James Monroe, were six years of age the family moved to a farm about three and a half miles south of Monroe City, Missouri. The year was 1851, probably the summer, a few months after the baby was born. A cholera epidemic had swept the nation in 1849. It is recorded as having caused many fatalities in the Indian Creek settlement in 1850. It is possible that the timing of the move was influenced by the epidemic.

Fielder had at least one brother from his immediate family who chose to move to the Indian Creek settlement, Cyprian. Whether they traveled at the same time, I do not know.

FROM KENTUCKY
TO MISSOURI

FIELDER'S FAMILY NEEDED TO TRAVEL A DISTANCE OF approximately 450 miles, taking with them all their belongings, necessary provisions, their animals, and of course, their hopes and dreams.

In 1851, what was called the Prairie Schooner became a frequent site. So named because the white canvas resembled the sail of a ship, it represented the Pioneer Spirit of America. While covered wagons were the preferred mode of travel, they were not exactly all that they would appear to be from western movies.

Only the very wealthy could afford two wagons, one to pack and one to sleep in. A larger wagon, the Conestoga wagon, required a team of six horses to pull, and horses were a luxury. As the typical schooner was no more than four feet wide and eight to nine feet long, it could be pulled by two mules or oxen that were also the needed farm animals.

The covered wagon had to be loaded carefully with the heavier, larger items on the bottom. Otherwise, a wagon could tip over rather easily. As breakdown of wood or metal parts occurred regularly, the wagon would often have to be completely emptied to repair the part.

The driver endured a jarring, rugged ride while the others walked or were carried beside the wagon. On a good day, the settlers might travel twenty miles. But obstacles such as weather, river crossings, and accidents occurred regularly. The white canvas was coated with linseed oil to make it as waterproof as possible. This canvass could be pulled tight on each end of the wagon during a storm. However, the refuge for the family was usually sleeping under the wagon. Exhaustion, accidents and disease took a toll.[63]

From sea to sea, America's overland trail was marked, not only by wagon tracks, but by graves of fallen family members who would be forever missed.

Kentucky borders Missouri on its southwestern tip, but only by crossing the Mississippi. Although I do not know the route that Fielder and his family took, crossing the Mississippi was usually by ferry in 1851. They probably took another ferry across the Missouri River. There were still smaller rivers they might have forded, or crossed at a shallow point. The journey would have occurred when the weather was most favorable, probably in the summer. The families who journeyed together for mutual support were at the mercy of nature. They had to be settled before winter. The journey itself lasted perhaps a month. But, afterwards, the family would have to live in temporary shelter, something hastily put together, while land was cleared and a permanent home was built.

The cost of this venture must have taken every cent they owned. Anything left after travelling would have been spent on land. It was most certainly a courageous journey.

Her family survived the wagon trek, but Harriet died later that same year, in 1851.

Per family records, she was buried on the family farm. However, another record indicates she was buried in St. Stephen's Cemetery. I was unable to locate her headstone, however her grave would have been located in the older section of the cemetery. That section was leveled by the cyclone of 1876 and broken pieces of stone markers resting on a carefully-tended concrete base are what is left.

The youngest child of Fielder, Mary Elizabeth, was baptized on August 8, 1851 at St. Stephen's Church.[64]

MARY C. (DONNALLY) HAGAN;
EIGHT STEP CHILDREN AND FOUR MORE

A WIDOWER WITH EIGHT CHILDREN WAS IN NEED OF THE support of his community. The older girls, no doubt, took on childcare of the younger ones and did the best they could with chores.

In nearby Ralls County, Cornelius Donnally (also spelled Donnelly) had taken the same route as the Hagan family. Also an Irish Catholic, he was born in Maryland and had traveled to Kentucky where his children were born. He eventually moved to Missouri. Upon his death he was buried in the cemetery near St. Peter's Catholic Church, less than 20 miles from Indian Creek. His daughter, Catherine, had married Thomas Spalding and settled in the Indian Creek settlement. Catherine's youngest sister was Mary C. Donnally. I do not know much about her, but she was, without a doubt, a woman of great courage and compassion.

In 1854, Mary C. was 32 years of age when she married Fielder who was about 38. She took on eight step children, the youngest was less than four. The following year she gave birth to their first child, Harriet Malinda, named no doubt after her husband's first wife. She eventually gave birth to three more children, adding to the family total of twelve. The youngest member of this family was my great grandfather, Richard Ledwith Hagan.

RICHARD LEDWITH
HAGAN

*From left to right, George Washington Hagan holding granddaughter,
Dorothy Ann Hagan, Fielder H. Hagan, James Monroe Hagan, Edward
Richard Hagan, and Richard Ledwith Hagan, photo taken about 1918*

R ICHARD LEDWITH HAGAN WAS, MOST LIKELY, GIVEN HIS MIDDLE
name after a priest, Rev. Thomas Ledwith, who served the St.
Stephen's Congregation from 1861 until 1863.

Born in 1863, he came into the world during the Civil War.

Missouri was a house divided during the Civil War. Although it officially remained a Union state, the Confederacy, at one time, also claimed it with a star on the Confederate flag. Governor Claiborne Fox Jackson was a confederate sympathizer who maintained an alternate secessionist state government for a time. Armies, generals, and supplies were sent to the opposing sides. Some Missouri families and neighbors were torn apart by the resulting strife.[65]

The Indian Creek community survived with only one recorded episode of bloodshed. This one episode was the only blot on the community that has survived these many years without a town marshal or a jail.

In 1864 Rufus Hayden got into an argument with his neighbor, Marcellus Abell, over secession. The argument ended with Hayden taking the life of Abell.[66] A nearby newspaper, *The Palmyra Spectator*, carried the story on June 17th, 1864.

Marcellus died shortly after the shooting and Rufus delivered himself up to the proper authorities. After an investigation, the authorities deemed the case one of justifiable homicide. Rufus was acquitted. Both Rufus Hayden and Marcellus Abell are buried in St. Stephen's cemetery.

Richard Ledwith Hagan married Malinda J. Hayden. Malinda gave birth to their daughter, Mary Bertha in 1886 when she was twenty years old. The little girl died at the age of fifteen months. Tragically, in 1890 Mary also died, less than three years after their daughter. They are buried side by side in the cemetery of St. Stephen's near Richard's father and mother. Richard's father had died the year before, in 1889.

BEAUTY FOR ASHES; CAROLINE "CARRIE" BELLE (BORDEN) HAGAN

Richard Ledwith Hagan and Carolyn "Carrie" Hagan

CAROLYN "CARRIE" BELLE BORDEN WAS THE DAUGHTER OF Isaac Addison Borden. Isaac was a confederate veteran of the Civil War who served under General Sterling J. Price.[67] Her mother was Clarissa Britanna Abell, who was from nearby Ralls County, Missouri. Isaac and Clarissa married after the war, in 1869.

Isaac was born in Massachusetts where he had family members. His brother, John, enlisted as a Union soldier in 1863.[68]

The Civil War was truly brother against brother.

Isaac and Clarissa knew the heartache of losing three children in infancy. This was during a time when children often did not survive until adulthood. Headstones of those who lived but a short time on this earth are marked not by years, but by the number of months and days they were on this earth. Two daughters survived until adulthood, Francis and Caroline, as well as at least one son, Ernest.

On January 17th, 1894, thirty year old Richard married "Carrie" Borden who was twenty-one. Like his fathers before him, he was a farmer. He also raised mules. Mules were the farm animal used most often in Missouri. A cross between a "jack", a male donkey, and a mare, a female horse, creates a tough, resilient work animal that is better suited than a horse to pull a plow or a wagon.

In time, Richard and Carrie had five children. Their eldest, a daughter, was my grandmother, Mary Leola Hagan. She was born in 1894.

MARY LEOLA (HAGAN) MONTGOMERY

From left to right: William Joseph "Joe" Hagan, Ernest Bernard Hagan, Mary Leola "Ola" Hagan, and Lillian "Lilly" Hagan. Not yet born was Clarissa Mabel Hagan.

*Ernest Bernard and Mary Leola Hagan at
high school graduation, about 1912*

M Y GRANDMOTHER "OLA" MET HER HUSBAND, JOSEPH Tibertious "Joe" Montgomery at church. His family had also travelled from Maryland to Kentucky to Missouri in hopes of a better life. My granddad's middle name came from the date he was born, August 11, 1894. August 11th is the Catholic feast day of Saint Tiburtious, a Roman, who was martyred for his faith in the third century.[69] Most people couldn't pronounce or spell Tibertius, so he went by Joseph T.

Whereas my grandmother was the eldest of five, my grandfather was the youngest of ten. His family had also come from a long line of farmers. His father, John Henry Montgomery, died when he was young. He and his brother Robert, my "Uncle Bob," were responsible for his mother, Mary Elizabeth (Pike) Montgomery. As a result, my grandparents married later than most, in 1927, when they were about thirty-three years of age. They had six children, including a baby, Wilfred Glennon, who died of pneumonia at seven months of age. In times prior to antibiotics, pneumonia was a common cause of death. I can still recall my grandmother's tears one day I was visiting. She was in her late seventies at the time.

We were talking of baby Wilfred and she was certain she had left him too close to an open window on a hot summer day. It didn't matter that everyone opened windows in August of 1932. She was still carrying the pain.

JOSEPH T. MONTGOMERY

Joseph T. and Mary Leola "Ola" (Hagan) Montgomery

St. Stephen's Catholic Church, Indian Creek, Missouri

Back row, from left to right: Melvin F. Montgomery, Mary Carolyn
(Montgomery) Hack, Rita Jo (Montgomery) Kendrick, and John R. Montgomery.
Front row, from left to right: Mary Leola (Hagan) Montgomery,
Dorothy (Montgomery) Dierker, and Joseph T. Montgomery

J OSEPH T. M ONTGOMERY CAME FROM A LONG LINE OF C ATHOLIC farmers who had essentially traveled the same ancestry trail as the Hagan family. In fact, his grandfather, Charles William Montgomery had also married a Hagan, perhaps a distant cousin, Helen Matilda Hagan. They had come from Springfield, Kentucky. In the generation prior to Charles, William Peter Montgomery, died at the age of 35 in the 1833 cholera epidemic.

John Henry Montgomery and Charles William Montgomery

The oldest known ancestor of the Montgomerys was Peter Montgomery who was believed to be from France. He bought land in Maryland in 1726 in Charles County, Maryland. The land is now about one-half mile from the Wicomico River which empties into the Potomac near the Chesapeake Bay. Charles, son of Peter, migrated to Kentucky in 1795.[70]

COUSINS

"**O**LA" AND "JOE" PROUDLY SPOKE OF THEIR 25 GRANDCHIL-
dren. My paternal grandfather worked as a farmer and an
insurance agent. Uncle Bob lived with my grandparents throughout
his life. They lived on a farm near Indian Creek, eventually moving to a home across the street from St. Stephen's Church. They
are buried side by side in the cemetery there, both passing away
in 1980.

As a child living in the same community with previous
generations, I could proudly recite all my cousins' names: Ed,
Bob, Tim, Susan, Jane, Glenn, Joe, Jeff, Gary, Beverly, David, Jim,
Marsha, Lori, Brian, Teresa, Scott, Anita, Keith and Annette. I now
realize everyone else in the community was simply a more distant
cousin. The names Hagan, Yeager, Hays, Spalding, Buckman,
Yates, as well as others reappear from one Catholic center to the
next. Because of shared values as well as persecution, Catholics had
moved westward from one center of worship to another. Attending
St. Stephen's Mass on Sunday was definitely a family affair.

To continue this story beyond my grandmother's generation
was more than my family records include or time will allow. Suffice
it to say we all learned the importance of family. We learned to lean
on faith in the hard times and always watch for God's surprises
when a door seems to close. It is this legacy of hope that we have
been left. It is this legacy that we intend to pass on.

LYNN M. MONTGOMERY

ENDNOTES

1   Henry Hagan, OSB., "Thomas and Mary Hagan of Charles Co., Maryland and Their Descendants in Central Kentucky to About 1850", June 1996, https.//www.yumpu.com/en/document/view/13414297/thomas-mary-hagan(accessed June 17,2020), 7.

2   "Historic St. Mary's City", https://hsmcdigshistory.org.(accessed Feb. 11, 2020).

3   "Red Legs in Barbados". *The Irish Times,* Saturday, January 17, 2009, http://www-irishtimes-com.cdn.ampproject.org (accessed Feb. 10, 2020).

4   Joseph M. Greeley, *Watery Highways: Trade and travel in the Colonial Chesapeake,* copyright 2005 Historic St. Mary's Commission, 24.

5   Sally M. Walker, *Ghost Walls; the Story of a 17th Century Colonial Homestead* (Minneapolis, MN: Carolrhoda Books, 2014), 16.

6   *Encyclopedia Britannica,* "Reformation/History, Summary, & Reformers", https://www.brittanica.com/event/Reformation, (accessed 15 June, 2020).

7   Walker, 13.

8   Walker, 14.

9   Walker, 15.

10 Silas D. Hurry "*. . . once the Metropolis of Maryland*" The History and Archeology of Maryland's First Capital. Copyright 2001 Historic St. Mary's Commission, 6-8.

11 "Exploring Maryland's Roots: Library: Father Andrew White (1579-1656)", http://mdroots.thinkport.org/library/andrewwhite.asp (accessed July 22, 2020).

12 "Maryland 2: The Ark and the Dove", September 5, 2018, http://americanhistorypodcast.net/maryland-2-the-ark-dove/, (accessed July 22, 2020).

13 "Feast of the Holy Cross", published September 14, 2014, https://cardinalsblog.adw.org/2014/09/14/feast-holy-cross/ (accessed July 30, 2020).

14 Hurry, 9-10.

15 Walker, 19.

16 Hurry, 11.

17 Walker, 47.

18 Hagan, 8.

19 Hurry, 24.

20 "Historic St. Mary's City" https://hsmcdigshistory.org, (accessed 17 Feb 2020).

21 Hagan, 9.

22 Hagan, 7.

23 Hagan, p.8.

24 Walker, 61.

25 Greeley, 28.

26 Walker, 69.

27 Walker, 67.

28 Henry Miller, HSMC Director of Research, "The Lure of Softweed: Tobacco and Maryland History" Historic St. Mary's City, https://hsmcdigshistory.org (accessed July 19 2020).

29 Walker, 45-46.

30 Greeley, 26-27.

31 Hurry, 8.

32 Timothy J. O'Rourke, *Maryland Catholics on the frontier: the Missouri and Texas settlements,* third printing 1993, (Brefney Press by the Parsons News, Parsons, Kansas), 548.

33 Walker, 52.

34 Walker, 51.

35 Hagan, 36.

36 Lloyd DeWitt Bockstruck, "Revolutionary War Bounty Land Grants; Reasons for Issuing Bounty Land Grants", https://www.genealogy.com/articles/research24_land.html (accessed July 19, 2020).

37 Neal O. Hammon "Early Kentucky Land Records 1773-1780", http://genealogy trails.com/vir/fincastle/fincastlecommissionerland.html, (accessed July 19, 2020).

38 O'Rourke, 1-2.

39 Hagan, 122.

40 "Wilderness Road", https://en.m.wikipedia.org/wiki/WildernessRoad (accessed 12 August, 2020).

41 Hagan, 116.

42 Hagan, 130-131.

43 *Basilica of St. Joseph Proto-Cathedral Bicentennial Celebration 1819-2019*, Published by the Kentucky Standard, (accessed August 11, 2019).

44 Sarah B. Smith, "Historic Nelson County, Its towns and People", (Published and Distributed by Nelson County Genealogical Roundtable, Bardstown, KY) 47.

45 Deborah Heal, "Flatboats on the Ohio River" Posted May 8, 2015, http://deborahheal.com/flatboats-ohio-river/ (accessed July 16, 2020).

46 Smith, 47.

47 Hagan, 39.

48 O'Rourke, 4.

49 Smith, 48.

50 "Benedict Joseph Flaget", https://en.m.wikipedia.org/wiki/Benedict Joseph Flaget (accessed 30 July 2020).

51 "Basilica of St. Joseph Proto-Cathedral", https://en.m.wikipedia.org/wiki/Basilica of St. Joseph pror Cathedral (accessed 7 August, 2020).

52 O'Rourke, 549.

53 "The Potato Famine and Irish Immigration to America", Constitutional Rights Foundation, Bill of Rights in Action, (winter 2010, Volume 26, No.2), https://www.crf-usa.org/bill-of-rights-in-action/bria-26-2-the-potato-famine-and-irish-immigration-to-america.html (accessed 7 August 2020).

54 "History of Missouri", https://en.m.wikipedia.org/wiki/History of Missouri (accessed 24 July 2020).

55 "Fenwick Settlement, Missouri", https://en.m.wikipedia.org/wiki/Fenwick Settlement Missouri (accessed 24 July 2020).

56 Hagan, 39.

57 O'Rourke, 2-3.

58 Louis LaCross, *St. Louis Globe Democrat,* Sunday, February 7th, 1926, Reprinted in *Swinkey Stories; 175 years of Memories,* booklet for 175th anniversary of St. Stephen's Church, Indian Creek, Missouri, 5.

59 Leslie Francis Pike, *Indian Creek Settlement 150 years; 1833-1983,* booklet printed for 150th anniversary of St. Stephen's Church, Indian Creek, Missouri, 14.

60 Pike, 7.

61 *Swinkey Stories: 175 Years of Memories, 3.*

62 Pike, 10-11.

63 Karen Harris, "8 Things You Didn't Know About Real-Life-Covered Wagons", May 24, 2019, https://historydaily.org/covered-wagons-facts-trivia-didn't-know (accessed 13 August 2020).

64 Pike, 23.

65 *The Kansas City Public Library,* "Civil War on the Western Border", https://civilwaronthewesternborder.org/border-war-encyclopedia (accessed September 13, 2020).

66 Pike, 45.

67 Confederate Veterans of Monroe County Missouri

68 Muster and Descriptive Roll of a Detachment of U.S. Vols. Forwarded, John J. Borden, 2 Cav., Massachusetts, Dec, 29, 1863, https://www.findagrave.com/memorial/30622290/john-j.-borden (accessed Sept 16 2020).

69 "Book of Saints-Tiburtius", https://catholicsaints.info/book-of-saints-tiburtius/ (accessed Sept 18, 2020).

70 Notes from historical data gathered by Thomas A. Montgomery and his wife, Ellen; Paul M. Montgomery and wife, Catherine; and James A. Montgomery

ABOUT THE AUTHOR

Lynn M. Montgomery is a retired registered nursing living in Lakeview, Arkansas. She is the ninth generation of the Hagan family journey told in this book. Her father is Melvin F. Montgomery, son of Mary Leola Hagan Montgomery. Her mother is Mary Anne Evans Montgomery. Brothers are Paul and David Montgomery. Her sisters are Lesa Montgomery Santoro and Sheila Montgomery Park.

Printed in the United States
By Bookmasters